Problem Solving Safari

MANIPULATIVES

Searching for opportunities to teach problem solving skills while working with manipulatives

AF892468

By Barbara F. Backer, M.Ed.
Illustrated by Gary Mohrman

Totline® Publications
A Division of Frank Schaffer Publications, Inc.
Torrance, California

In loving memory of my father, Leon H. Feldman.

—B.F.B.

Managing Editor: Kathleen Cubley
Editor: Gayle Bittinger
Contributing Editors: Carol Gnojewski, Susan Hodges, Elizabeth McKinnon, Jean Warren
Copyeditor: Kris Fulsaas
Proofreader: Miriam Bulmer
Editorial Assistant: Durby Peterson
Graphic Designer: Gordon Frazier
Graphic Designer (Cover): Brenda Mann Harrison
Production Manager: Melody Olney

ISBN: 1-57029-121-7

Printed in the United States of America
Published by Totline® Publications
Editorial Office: P.O. Box 2250
Everett, WA 98203
Business Office: 23740 Hawthorne Blvd.
Torrance, CA 90505

20 19 18 17 16 15 14 13 12 11 10 9 8 7 6 5 4 3 2

INTRODUCTION

Young children learn many concepts just by "messing around" with manipulative materials. These can be purchased items like blocks that snap together in various ways, puzzles, magnets, pegs and pegboards, or household items like bottle tops, jar lids, discarded keys, or a variety of buttons. Concepts your children can learn range from discovering cause and effect to deciding what to do when there aren't enough blocks to go around.

When young children play with manipulative toys, problem solving opportunities frequently arise. The purpose of this book is to help teachers become more aware of these opportunities when they set up their manipulative toys area. These opportunities can challenge children's critical thinking skills as they analyze a problem and decide what to do. Children stretch their capacity for creative thinking as they combine ideas in new ways.

In *Problem Solving Safari—Manipulatives*, 20 scenarios are presented, each centering around a particular problem. These realistic problems, with their possible solutions, come from children's real play and reflect their point of view. The problems provide springboards for children to become creative and discover how or why things work. Various problem solving steps are suggested to help your children identify problems and then brainstorm workable solutions. Your role in encouraging this process is outlined as well. There are no right or wrong solutions—all the children's ideas are respected. If they try to solve a problem and it does not work, this too becomes a valuable learning experience. It allows them to analyze and evaluate a solution, then try again.

To stretch your children's thinking skills, a list of children's books about the concepts explored through manipulative toys is provided. Also, a reproducible Parent Flyer is included to use as an invitation for parents to become a part of the learning process and join their children as they observe and explore.

Problem Solving Safari—Manipulatives describes many open-ended opportunities to arouse your children's curiosity, encourage their creativity, promote their critical thinking and social interactions, and strengthen their physical abilities. All of these opportunities provide an important beginning for the development of your children's problem solving skills.

CONTENTS

STEPS FOR PROBLEM SOLVING

Below are steps that you can take with your children when determining problems, developing solutions, and putting those solutions into action.

1. **IDENTIFY** – Determine and discuss the problem. It should be meaningful, interesting, and appropriate for young children.

2. **BRAINSTORM** – Encourage your children to think about possible solutions. Listen to and respect all of their ideas. Keep a record of the solutions suggested in case the children want to try more than one.

3. **SELECT** – Help your children examine the advantages and disadvantages of various solutions and then choose one that seems workable.

4. **EXPLORE AND IMPLEMENT** – Let your children gather the necessary materials and resources and then try out the solution they decided upon.

5. **EVALUATE** – With your children, observe and discuss whether the solution to the problem was successful. If appropriate, help the children think of changes they might want to make in the idea they tried. Or, encourage them to try other solutions.

YOUR ROLE

Your role in facilitating the development of your children's problem solving behaviors is that of encourager and guide. Be sure to allow plenty of time and space for the children to brainstorm and to try out their ideas. Below are other ways you can help.

- Listen to, acknowledge, and support your children's ideas. Respect their suggestions and encourage them to value one another's viewpoints.
- Provide easy access to stimulating materials. If your children need assistance, help them learn how to use the materials in diverse ways.
- Arouse curiosity. Ask open-ended questions that begin with "What if?" or "Why do you suppose?" to foster creative—and critical—thinking.
- Encourage experimentation. Let your children know that it is all right to take a guess or try a new idea (always keeping in mind the children's safety). Help them understand that there are no "perfect" solutions.
- Observe carefully to see how you can facilitate the problem solving process. For instance, provide or add special materials when needed. Also, encourage your children to observe in order to verify what is happening.
- Turn any mistake into a learning experience. Help your children analyze why a solution did not work out.
- Promote discussion, interaction, and collaboration. As your children work together, help them to be patient and persistent in their explorations.
- Throughout the day, model problem solving skills in natural ways. However, avoid solving your children's problems for them. Trust them to come up with solutions!

STRINGING BEADS

Your children are stringing beads onto long laces. They decide they want to make necklaces. How can they do this?

Children's Possible Solutions	Your Role
1. A child picks up one end of his string of beads. As he lifts the string, the beads slide off the other end. He wraps many layers of masking tape around the far end of the string, making it so thick that the beads cannot slip off. Now he strings beads again, then brings the string to you to tie into a necklace.	Compliment the child on his problem solving technique.
2. Another child has two strings knotted together and the knot holds her beads on the first string. When she holds the ends together around her neck, the necklace is much too long and one string has no beads on it.	Watch and wait to see if the child wants help. Encourage her attempts to discover a solution.

Extending the Experience

- Ask parents to donate used shoelaces to use in stringing activities. Challenge your children to find items to string. Old keys work well.
- Dye stringable pasta by placing 1 cup of pasta in a plastic jar with 1 tablespoon of rubbing alcohol and 1 teaspoon of food coloring. Screw on the lid and shake well. Spread the pasta pieces on waxed paper to dry. Let your children string them on shoelaces or yarn.

STIFF PAPER PUNCHES

Your children are using the paper punches to make sewing cards. Two of the punches are stiff and difficult to work. What can the children do?

Children's Possible Solutions	Your Role
1. Several children take their punches to the sink and run water on them. "The punches feel too dry," they explain.	Encourage the children's efforts and compliment them on their idea. Discuss the results.
2. One child has seen the teacher rub petroleum jelly on the insides of paint container lids to keep them from sticking to the containers. She wants to rub petroleum jelly on the hole punch.	Provide materials and support the child's efforts. Discuss the results. What are the advantages and disadvantages of this method?
3. Another child has seen his mom squirt oil on things (sewing machine parts, a stiff door hinge) to make them move smoothly. He wants an oil can so he can put a drop of oil in the punches' joints.	Compliment the child for applying a workable idea that he observed elsewhere. Supply the oil if you have it. If not, brainstorm to see if you have a possible substitute.

Extending the Experience

- Show your children how oil acts as a lubricant to help metal parts move smoothly over one another. Together, find a squeaky hinge to oil.
- Make collages with the paper punchouts.

JAR LIDS AND BOTTLE TOPS

Your children have collected jar lids and bottle tops to see how many it would take to fill a special box. The whole class has counted 246 lids and tops. Now, what can they do with these?

Children's Possible Solutions	Your Role
1. Some children take a pile of lids and separate them into two stacks, one for rough lids and one for smooth ones. They run their fingers over the raised lettering on some of the lids to show you where they are "rough."	Compliment the children on their thinking. Ask if there are other ways they might group the lids.
2. One girl sorts some of the lids by color. She gets a container of teddy bear counters and puts a matching-colored teddy bear on each colored lid. She looks for a long time at the metallic lids, then she smiles and jumps up to get a container of keys. She puts a matching-colored metal key onto each lid.	Congratulate the child on her colorful solution.
3. Two children lay tops and lids in two parallel lines that curve about, leaving enough room between the lines for a small car to roll through. "We're making a road," one of them says.	Admire the children's work, and if they want to add intersections and side roads, discuss ways they might do so.

Extending the Experience

- Find rough and smooth items and place them in separate piles.
- Explore with several colors of teddy bear counters and matching-colored strips of paper.

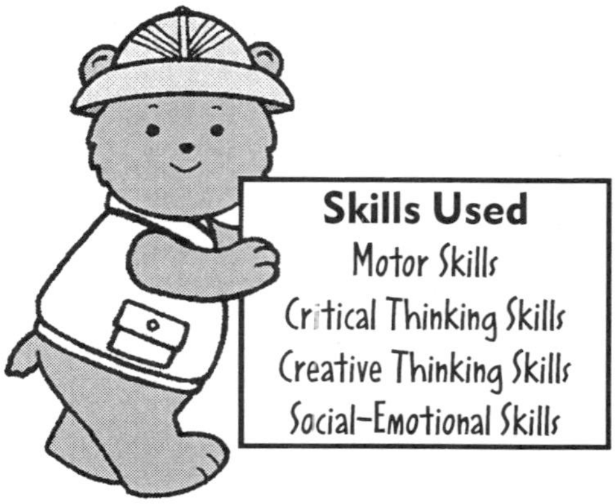

LOTS OF LETTERS

Several children have gathered wooden, plastic, and magnetic letters, as well as the letter cards from an alphabet game. They would like to play a game with all these letters. What game can they make up?

Children's Possible Solutions	Your Role
1. Two children lay out the letter cards and bring objects from the room to put on each letter. "Bring a truck for *T*," one child says.	Admire the children's work. If they cannot think of items for some letters, suggest they look in ABC books for ideas.
2. One child takes wooden letters to the art center. He traces the letters of his name, cuts them out, and pastes them to a sheet of construction paper.	Provide materials for children who want to copy the child's idea.
3. Some children put the magnetic letters on the side of a metal file cabinet. They sing the alphabet song, finding the letters as they go, putting them in order on the cabinet.	Watch quietly.

Extending the Experience

- Dip sponge letters onto paint pads and then press them onto paper to make letter prints.
- Walk, hop, or skip on large letters outlined on the floor with masking tape or drawn in the dirt outdoors.
- Fill the library area with a variety of ABC books.

TOO MANY CARDS

Several children are playing with a deck of cards, drawing from each other's hands and matching pairs. They are having trouble holding their cards. What can they do?

Children's Possible Solutions	Your Role
1. One child lays her cards face-up on the floor. Now she can see all of them, but so can the other children. Suddenly she is losing all of her cards as the others choose exactly what they want.	Compliment the child on her solution. Brainstorm ways she could hide her cards from others.
2. Another child also lays his cards face-up on the floor, but first he stands two tall books on end so they hide his cards. When someone wants to select a card, he picks up his cards, holds them out, and then, after the selection has been made, spreads them out behind the books again.	Comment on the child's creative thinking. Ask what the others think of this idea.
3. A girl takes two clothespins from the art center. She divides her cards into two groups and fans out each group. She clips a clothespin onto each group. When other players point to the cards they want, she removes them from the clothespins.	Praise the child's problem solving skills.

Extending the Experience

- Arrange numbered cards in order from one to ten.
- When two or more decks of playing cards get mixed together, have your children sort them.
- Make up new games using old playing cards.

RAINBOW PEGS

Several children are playing with pegboards and pegs. A girl is putting "candles" on a cake. One of the boys is making a rainbow. They both want more red pegs. What happens now?

Children's Possible Solutions	Your Role
1. The boy cries, "Give me the red pegs. The girl refuses to relinquish any red pegs. The boy whines, "Teacher, make her give me her red pegs."	Watch carefully to see what occurs. Be ready to step in if needed.
2. The girl counts the empty holes in the boy's row of red pegs. There are four. She looks at his other pegs and announces, "I'll give you four red pegs if you give me six purple pegs and three green pegs. I need them for my birthday cake." The boy checks his rainbow to see if he needs those other pegs, then agrees to the trade.	Praise the children for their peaceful solution.

Extending the Experience

- Explore with modeling dough and pegs.
- Divide your children into pairs. Give each pair one pegboard and some pegs. Let them work together to create a design.

Skills Used
Social-Emotional Skills
Motor Skills
Creative Thinking Skills

NO THROWING ALLOWED

While your children are playing with blocks, one child throws a block at another child. The other children don't like this. What can they do?

Children's Possible Solutions	Your Role
1. One girl thinks that any toys that are thrown should be put in the closet so no one can play with them.	Ask what the other children think of this idea. Brainstorm other options.
2. A boy suggests a rule: No throwing blocks at school.	Encourage discussion. Offer materials if the children want to make "Do not throw" signs to put in the block area.
3. Other children say that if they want to throw things, they should go outside and throw balls.	Let your children go outside and throw balls if they want.

Extending the Experience

- Have a group meeting to go over classroom rules.
- Talk about where and what your children can throw. Let them demonstrate and practice this.
- Outside, toss balls through a Hula Hoop hanging from a tree branch or a clothesline.

THESE PEOPLE DON'T LOOK LIKE ME!

Several children are playing with the dollhouse. One boy, who uses a walker, says, "Hey, there's no walker in this house." A girl, who wears glasses, notices that none of the toy people wear glasses. They want to change this. How?

Children's Possible Solutions	Your Role
1. The boy gets pipe cleaners from the art center and begins fashioning a walker.	Encourage the child's efforts.
2. The girl, who is blonde, takes a pen and begins drawing glasses on a dark-haired figure. "Hey," shouts a brunette girl, "That one is me. Put glasses on this one." She hands her a blonde figure.	Be ready to mediate disputes. Support both girls' efforts. Discuss other ways to add glasses besides writing on toys.

Extending the Experience

- Find a magazine picture to represent each child. Cut out the pictures, mount them on heavy paper, cover them with clear self-stick paper, and put them in the manipulatives toy area.
- Add a variety of multiethnic, differently abled figures to your dollhouse. Have your children help you select these from school supply catalogs.

THIS PUZZLE IS TOO HARD

A boy has been sitting on the floor working with a tray puzzle that has many pieces. He is unable to complete it and is feeling frustrated. He doesn't want to work on the puzzle anymore. What can he do?

Children's Possible Solutions	Your Role
1. The boy angrily stacks the puzzle pieces on the tray and carries them to the shelf. A child sees him and tells him he can't put the puzzle away like that.	Do not intervene, but watch carefully to see that tempers do not get out of hand.
2. One girl notices his frustration and says, "I'll put it together for you."	Suggest that the girl show him *how* to put the puzzle together. As she works, describe her actions: "She puts the biggest pieces in first. She looks for a piece that is the same color as this."

Extending the Experience

- Glue large color copies of your children's photos to heavy paper. Cover each one with clear self-stick paper, cut it into puzzle pieces, and place it in a separate resealable bag. Children love putting together these "friendly" puzzles.
- Offer a variety of puzzles for varying skill levels to encourage successful puzzle experiences for everyone.

Skills Used
Social-Emotional Skills
Motor Skills
Critical Thinking Skills

NOT ENOUGH BUILDING LOGS

Three children have been creating with the building logs. They decide to build a city. "We need more logs," they say. They look around the classroom. There are no more logs. What can they do?

Children's Possible Solutions	Your Role
1. One child suggests bringing some from home.	Brainstorm ways of marking and counting the logs the children bring from home so they will take home the same logs that they bring.
2. Some children think they should use cardboard tubes. They can tape them together.	Make these materials available.
3. Another child suggests asking other classrooms if they can borrow their building logs.	Allow the children to go to other classrooms and to ask the teachers if they can borrow their logs. Again, decide how to count and mark the logs so they can all be returned to the correct classrooms.

Extending the Experience

- Roll grocery bags lengthwise to make "logs" and secure the ends with masking tape. Fasten these together with glue, rubber bands, or masking tape to build structures.
- Team up with other teachers and share materials from room to room. One week you have all of the building logs and the other class has all of the interlocking blocks.

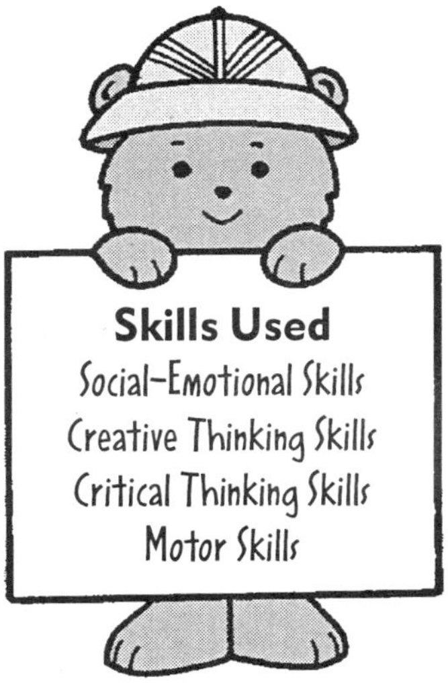

JUMPING PAPER CLIPS

Two children are playing with magnets and an assortment of paper clips. One boy is holding six disc magnets stacked together in one hand. As he passes his hand a few inches above the clips, a few of them seem to "jump" up to his hand. The children want to know why this is happening. What can they do?

Children's Possible Solutions	Your Role
1. Some children try passing their empty hands over the paper clips. Nothing happens.	Encourage discussion of the children's observations. What is different about the two situations?
2. The boy passes his "magnet" hand over the paper clips a second time, only this time his hand is farther away. Nothing happens. When he lowers his hand, the paper clips jump up again.	Support the child's actions. What does he think is happening?
3. Another child has been watching carefully. She passes a stack of ten disc magnets over the clips. Many clips jump high toward the magnets and several stick to them. She stacks all the remaining magnets together, passes them over the clips, and watches the clips jump even higher.	Praise the child's observations and logical thinking.

Extending the Experience

- Explore a variety of magnets including refrigerator magnets; small, strong magnets from a hardware store; horseshoe magnets; and so on.
- Place paper clips in a jar of water and screw on the lid. Provide magnets and encourage exploration.
- Place several small magnetic and nonmagnetic items in a shallow, plastic box with a clear lid. Move a strong magnet across the lid and observe the materials inside.

THE TRAVELING VOICE

Several children are playing with cardboard tubes of various sizes. Using funny voices, they are talking into one end of their tubes and pointing the tubes in various directions. They want to experiment with making their voices sound like they are coming from different places. How can they do this?

Children's Possible Solutions	Your Role
1. One boy stands in front of a girl and holds his long tube so that one end is behind her ear. When he talks, his voice sounds as if it is coming from behind her.	Compliment the child on his experiment. Soon everyone will want long tubes. Encourage children to develop a fair plan so each will get a turn using the longest tubes. (Remind your children to stand still and not run or play while the tubes are by their faces.)
2. Several children with long tubes hide behind a room divider. They stick the ends of their tubes out the sides of the divider. With silly voices, they talk into the tubes causing the children on the other side to burst into giggles when they hear sounds coming from a place where they see no children.	Join in the giggles provided by this inventive game.

Extending the Experience

- Use long, extra-sturdy cardboard tubes outdoors. (Sometimes carpet stores or upholstery fabric stores will have these tubes to donate.)
- Experiment with megaphones. These can be store-bought ones or ones you have made from the tops of 2-liter plastic bottles.
- Talk into a microphone.

Skills Used
Critical Thinking Skills
Creative Thinking Skills
Motor Skills
Social-Emotional Skills

SEASHELLS

Your children are playing with seashells, lining them up to make designs, then classifying them according to size and color. Some of the shells have holes in them. What can the children do with these?

Children's Possible Solutions	Your Role
1. One child gathers up several of the shells with holes. He takes them to the art center, where he strings them on yarn for a necklace.	Support the child's creative efforts. If the shells are needed in the manipulatives toy area, suggest that he unstring his necklace at the end of the day and return the shells.
2. Several children think the shells look like boats. They take the shells to the water table to float them, but after a few seconds they fill up with water and sink.	Compliment the children on their creative idea. Discuss the results. Is there any way they could make the shells more seaworthy? Evaluate any chosen solutions with your children.

Extending the Experience

- Add shells and a fishing net to the water table or shells and a sieve to the sand table.
- Set out shells in the art center for painting, coloring, or gluing on collages.

Skills Used
Critical Thinking Skills
Creative Thinking Skills
Motor Skills
Social-Emotional Skills

OPPOSITES

During circle time your children play a movement game about opposites, making themselves wide, then narrow; short, then tall; fast, then slow. They are excited about their discovery of opposites and want to explore this new concept during their free play time. How can they do this?

Children's Possible Solutions	Your Role
1. One child paints at the easel, making a pattern of wide lines and narrow lines.	Provide materials. Offer to label the child's finished work. Encourage him to hang the creation where others can see it.
2. Other children decide to start a collection of large and small items. They find a large paper clip and a small one, a child's shoe and a doll's shoe, a large wooden letter and a small magnetic letter, a new pencil and a pencil stub, and so on.	Compliment the children on their idea and their resourcefulness. Provide a place to display the collection and offer to help them label it.

Extending the Experience

- Show opposites by moving fast and slow, climbing up and down, and walking backward and forward.
- Take photos of your children walking up and down steps, standing right-side-up and hanging upside-down on the climbing bars, and standing near and far. Use the photos to make a book of opposites.

Skills Used
Critical Thinking Skills
Motor Skills
Creative Thinking Skills
Social-Emotional Skills

WHO HAS MORE?

Two children are playing with wooden unit cubes. Both children stack their cubes, and the stacks are the same height—nine cubes tall. They knock down their towers and one child's cubes scatter over a wider area than the other child's. The children want to know if they still have the same number of cubes. What can they do?

Children's Possible Solutions	Your Role
1. Both children count their cubes. They each have nine.	Help the children with the counting, if necessary.
2. One child says, "My blocks take up more room on the floor, so I must have more."	Encourage the children to lay the cubes on the floor side by side or ask them if they would like to compare their cubes by weighing them on the balance scale.
3. Both children stack up their blocks again and compare the height of their towers.	Ask the children what they observe. Encourage them to count the cubes in each stack. Evaluate any chosen solutions with your children.

Extending the Experience

- Count and compare numbers of things.
- Divide your children into two equal groups. Count each group. Have them line up facing each other. Count both groups. Have one group spread out. Count both groups again. Discuss the results.

Skills Used
Critical Thinking Skills
Motor Skills
Creative Thinking Skills
Social-Emotional Skills

THE SLANTED FLOOR

When your children play with small balls or marbles indoors, the balls always roll in one direction on the classroom floor, ending up by one wall. How can they incorporate this into their play?

Children's Possible Solutions	Your Role
1. One child blocks the rolling marble with her hand and pushes it back to the starting point. When she lets go, the marble again rolls toward the wall.	Support the child's action. Discuss her results.
2. Some children get a shoebox and set it against the wall. They take turns trying to roll marbles into the box "target."	Provide materials. Praise the children for their creative idea. Encourage others who want to make targets from different materials.

Extending the Experience

- Brainstorm ways to make targets outside to use with balls.
- Use a rubber ball to test different areas of the play yard to see which ones are level.

Skills Used
Creative Thinking Skills
Motor Skills
Critical Thinking Skills
Social-Emotional Skills

WHO LIVES ON THIS FARM?

Several children are playing with a small farm set—a barn, various toy animals, and a toy "farmer" figure. The children want to have the farmer's children feed the animals, but there are no child figures. What can they do?

Children's Possible Solutions	Your Role
1. A girl takes a slot-type clothespin and felt tip markers from the art center. She draws a face and clothes on the clothespin. The clothespin child "feeds" the animals.	Compliment the girl on her creative solution. Support her decision to use art materials in the manipulatives toy area.
2. A boy makes "people" from spools. Another cuts pictures of children from a magazine and tapes them to blocks.	Provide needed materials and compliment the children on their creations.

Extending the Experience

- Sing "Old MacDonald Had a Farm," but instead of singing about the sounds the animals make, sing about the foods they eat.
- Read books about farms. Talk about what the various animals eat.
- Visit a farm, if possible. Ask if the children can help feed the animals.

Skills Used
Creative Thinking Skills
Motor Skills
Social-Emotional Skills

PIRATE LIGHTS

Some children are under a table, playing with flashlights. One child suggests they make a pirate ship and use the flashlights to send signals to other pirate ships. How can they do this?

Children's Possible Solutions	Your Role
1. The children cover the table with a plastic tablecloth from the art area and a blanket from the dramatic play area. They hide in their new "ship."	Encourage the children's creative play by providing materials and by supporting their decision to use materials from more than one center.
2. Two children go to the block area and build a block ship.	Join in the excitement of having pirate ships in the room.
3. One child arranges two chairs for his ship and covers them with a transparent red scarf from the dramatic play area. When he flashes his signal, it looks red.	Point out the color of the child's signal light. Compliment him on his colorful idea.

Extending the Experience

- Turn out the classroom lights and use flashlights for reading, art, dramatic play, and other activities.
- Hold flashlights while doing movement activities. Enjoy the pattern of dancing lights.

THE CIRCUS

The circus is in town and many of your children have attended the performances. They want to create a circus in the manipulatives toy area. How can they do this?

Children's Possible Solutions	Your Role
1. They use blocks and other small manipulatives to build three rings for the circus. They put teddy bear counters and small plastic animals in the rings and use toy people as animal trainers.	Encourage the children's creative manipulations. Discuss the work of people and animals.
2. Two children want to make a trapeze. They build a standing crossbar from some building toys and hang a pipe cleaner trapeze from it.	Provide circus music to add an authentic atmosphere.
3. Some children want to make a circus tent. They place classroom chairs in a circle and drape a sheet over the chairs. They place zoo animals from the block area into shoebox cages around the outside of the tent.	Take photos of the finished creations inside and outside the tent. Include the creators in the photos. Encourage children who want to put these into a photo album along with dictated captions.

Extending the Experience

- Prepare popcorn and lemonade to "sell" at a "concession stand." Use art center supplies to make money for the concession stand.
- Let your children make up and star in their own circus. Provide materials for simple costumes or have them use props from the dramatic play area.

Skills Used
Creative Thinking Skills
Motor Skills
Social-Emotional Skills

BROKEN PUZZLES

Some of the tray puzzles have pieces missing. The children think they aren't good for puzzles anymore, but they don't want to throw them away. What can the children do with them?

Children's Possible Solutions	Your Role
1. One child wants to fix one of the puzzles by drawing in the missing pieces. She shows how by putting in all the remaining pieces, and then coloring the empty spaces on the puzzle tray with a felt tip marker.	Support the child's effort. Supervise carefully while you allow her to color in missing spaces.
2. Another child suggests getting rid of all the puzzle pieces and using the empty trays as building platforms in the block area.	Lead the children in a discussion of this solution.
3. Other children collect all the full-figure pieces (a Papa Bear, three bowls, and a chair) and take them to the dollhouse to play with them there.	Compliment the children on their original thinking.

Extending the Experience

- Add new puzzles to the manipulatives area. Encourage discussion about caring for the puzzles.
- Make a puzzle by folding a sheet of paper in half and cutting out a shape through the fold. Open the paper to discover a "puzzle tray" and a cut-out puzzle piece.
- Find other toys with missing pieces. What can the children do with these?

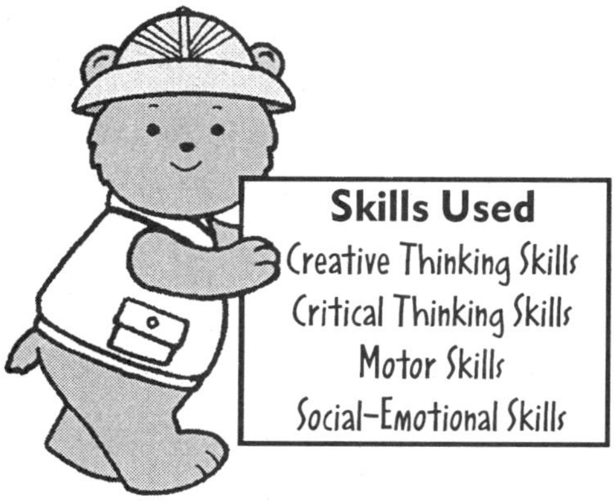

Parent Flyer

PROBLEM SOLVING WITH MANIPULATIVES

Young children learn many concepts just by manipulating their environment.

Experimenting with inexpensive or recycled materials like bottle caps or discarded keys allows children to discover how things are the same and how they are different. Purchased items like blocks that snap together, puzzles, and magnets and other manipulative materials lead to learning about cause and effect, size, shape, and space.

Look around you for problem solving opportunities such as those that follow. Then, with your child, have fun following the problem solving steps below to arrive at possible solutions. Remember, we all learn through trial and error; there are no "perfect" answers!

Problem Solving Opportunities

Below are some problems you and your child might encounter while playing with manipulatives together.

- This puzzle is missing a piece. Do we have to throw the puzzle away, or can we fix it?
- What else can I do with these refrigerator magnets?
- Who has the most snap-together blocks? How can we find out?
- What games can we make up using these old game boards?

Problem Solving Steps

Here are some simple problem solving steps to follow. Let your child take the lead; avoid solving the problem for your child.

1. Identify and discuss the problem.
2. Brainstorm ideas for solutions.
3. Select a solution that seems workable.
4. Try out the idea.
5. Evaluate your solution. If it didn't work, try another one.

CHILDREN'S BOOK LIST

Children learn about concepts by manipulating their environment. These books offer your children opportunities to learn about and discuss various these concepts.

The Accidental Zucchini, Max Grover. Browndeer Press, 1993. Objects like "apple autos," "ice-cream islands," and "vegetable volcanoes" illustrate the alphabet.

African Animals ABC, Philippa-Alys Browne. Sierra Club, 1995. African animals illustrate the alphabet.

Alphabet Puzzle, Jill Downie. Illus. by author. Lothrop, Lee & Shepard, 1988. Readers look through windows on the pages for hints of the pictures that represent the alphabet.

Amazon ABC, Kathy Darling. Photos by Tara Darling. Lothrop, Lee & Shepard, 1996. This book uses the alphabet as it guides readers through the beauty and diversity of the Amazon Rain Forest.

Balancing Act, A Counting Song, Illus. by Merle Peek. Clarion Books, 1987. The reader counts to ten as one elephant after another walks onto the high wire.

Blue Sea, Robert Kalan. Illus. by Donald Crews. Greenwillow, 1979. Various sizes of fish demonstrate concepts of spatial relationship and size.

Changes, Changes, Pat Hutchins. Macmillan, 1971. In this wordless book, two wooden figures have adventures as they transform their collection of table blocks. Conservation of number is demonstrated because the same blocks are rearranged for each construction.

Color: A Poem, Christina Rossetti. Illus. by Mary Teichman. HarperCollins, 1992. This book provides a simple introduction to colors and poetry.

Demi's Opposites, Demi. Grosset & Dunlap, 1987. In bold, double-page spreads, children explore opposite concepts such as open and shut, noisy and quiet, and curly and straight.

Is It Larger? Is It Smaller? Tana Hoban. Greenwillow, 1985. Photos of large and small animals and objects invite comparison of the two concepts.

Is It Rough? Is It Smooth? Is It Shiny? Tana Hoban. Greenwillow, 1984. In this wordless book, color photos show objects of many different textures.

Numbers, John J. Reiss. Bradbury Press, 1971. Colorful pictures provide opportunities to count from one to twenty and then, by tens, up to one hundred.

One Cow Coughs, Christine Loomis. Illus. by Pat Dypold. Tichnor & Fields Books for Young Readers, 1994. Readers count from one to ten and back down again as the barnyard animals become sick, treat their ills, and become well again.

Push-Pull, Empty-Full, Tana Hoban. Macmillan, 1972. Black and white photos illustrate opposites.

What Am I? N. N. Charles. Illus. by Leo and Diane Dillon. The Blue Sky Press, 1994. Rhyming questions and illustrations with cutout shapes introduce shapes, colors, and fruit.

Teacher Resources

from Totline® Publications

Celebrations

Easy, practical ideas for celebrating holidays and special days around the world. Plus ideas for making ordinary days special.

Celebrating Likes and Differences
Small World Celebrations
Special Day Celebrations
Great Big Holiday Celebrations

Theme-A-Saurus®

Classroom-tested, around-the-curriculum activities organized into imaginative units. Great for implementing a child-directed program.

Multisensory Theme-A-Saurus
Theme-A-Saurus
Theme-A-Saurus II
Toddler Theme-A-Saurus
Alphabet Theme-A-Saurus
Nursery Rhyme Theme-A-Saurus
Storytime Theme-A-Saurus

1•2•3 Series

Open-ended, age-appropriate, cooperative, and no-lose experiences for working with preschool children.

1•2•3 Art
1•2•3 Games
1•2•3 Colors
1•2•3 Puppets
1•2•3 Reading & Writing
1•2•3 Rhymes, Stories & Songs
1•2•3 Math
1•2•3 Science
1•2•3 Shapes

Snacks Series

Easy, educational recipes for healthy eating and expanded learning.

Super Snacks
Healthy Snacks
Teaching Snacks
Multicultural Snacks

Piggyback® Songs

New songs sung to the tunes of childhood favorites. No music to read! Easy for adults and children to learn. Chorded for guitar or autoharp.

Piggyback Songs
More Piggyback Songs
Piggyback Songs for Infants & Toddlers
Piggyback Songs in Praise of God
Piggyback Songs in Praise of Jesus
Holiday Piggyback Songs
Animal Piggyback Songs
Piggyback Songs for School
Piggyback Songs to Sign
Spanish Piggyback Songs
More Piggyback Songs for School

Busy Bees

These seasonal books help two- and three-year-olds discover the world around them through their senses. Each book includes fun activity and learning ideas, songs, snack ideas, and more!

Busy Bees—SPRING
Busy Bees—SUMMER
Busy Bees—FALL
Busy Bees—WINTER

101 Tips for Directors

Great ideas for managing a preschool or daycare. These hassle-free, handy hints are a great help.

Staff and Parent Self-Esteem
Parent Communication
Health and Safety
Marketing Your Center
Resources for You and Your Center
Child Development Training

101 Tips for Toddler Teachers

Designed for adults who work with toddlers.

Classroom Management
Discovery Play
Dramatic Play
Large Motor Play
Small Motor Play
Word Play

101 Tips for Preschool Teachers

Valuable, fresh ideas for adults who work with young children.

Creating Theme Environments
Encouraging Creativity
Developing Motor Skills
Developing Language Skills
Teaching Basic Concepts
Spicing Up Learning Centers

Problem Solving Safari

This unique series teaches teachers to help children problem-solve and think for themselves. Each book includes scenarios from children's real play and possible solutions.

Problem Solving Safari—Art
Problem Solving Safari—Blocks
Problem Solving Safari—Dramatic Play
Problem Solving Safari—Manipulatives
Problem Solving Safari—Outdoors
Problem Solving Safari—Science

The Best of Totline® Series

Collections of some of the finest, most useful material published in *Totline Magazine* over the years.

The Best of Totline
The Best of Totline Parent Flyers